Be That Man

R.C. Francis

Published by CMMprint
United Kingdom

Copyright © 2003 Rupert Colin Francis

All rights Reserved. Written permission must be secured from the publisher to use or reproduce any part of this book except for brief quotations.

Published in the United Kingdom by CMMprint (www.cmmprint.com) Unless otherwise indicated, all scripture Quotations are taken from the King James Version of the Bible. (KJV).

Scripture quotations noted NIV are taken from the Holy Bible NEW INTERNATIONAL VERSION Copyright © 1973. 1978, 1984 by International Bible Society. Used by permission.

Scripture quotations marked (TLB) are taken from *The Living Bible* copyright © 1971. Used by permission of Tyndale House Publishers, Inc., Wheaton, IL 60189. All rights reserved.

Scripture quotation noted TAB are taken from THE AMPLIFIED BIBLE, Copyright © 1954, 1958, 1962, 1964, 1965, 1987 by the Lockman Foundation. All rights reserved, Used by permission. (www.Lockman.org)

Scripture quotations noted CEV are taken from the Contemporary English Version of the Bible. Copyright © 1995 Thomas Nelson, Inc publishers. Used by permission. All rights reserved.

ISBN 0-9546816-0-6

Published by CMM Print
United Kingdom
E-mail: sales@cmmprint.com
Website: www.cmmprint.com

CONTENTS

Personal acknowledgement 4

Preface 6

Chapter 1 - God's Creative Act 10

Chapter 2 – Reflecting the Heavenly Father 16

Chapter 3 – Take Your Place as Head of the Family
And Trust God for the Grace You Need 20

Chapter 4 – Spiritual Maturity in the Family and Home 24

Chapter 5 – Living under an Open Heaven in your home 28

Chapter 6 – Jesus The Pattern For Authentic Manhood 32

Chapter 7 – A Special Message To Men Everywhere 34

                   Prayer – Your Kind Of Man 35

Chapter 8 – Making a Difference Means You
Must Be Born Again 38

Chapter 9 – The effect that submission to God
Has on our sphere of influence 42

Chapter 10 – Ten Commandments…Ten challenges 46

Conclusion 52

Prayer Section - Prayer To Be A Man Of God 54
                - Prayer For Your Wife 55
                - Prayer For Your Children 56

A Special Letter 58

To obtain further copies of this book 60

PERSONAL ACKNOWLEDGEMENT

I want to give God thanks for giving me such a beautiful, encouraging and supportive wife. When God brings two people together, he does it well. I also want to thank God for my beautiful daughter who has brought so much pleasure to my life. But I want you to know that it has not always been easy.

God, through this union, has helped me to reshape my life. We were not even a year into our marriage when we found ourselves arguing over the most ridiculous things. I found a person in me that I did not even know existed. I would flare up at the least provocation. I would shout a lot, throw things, and sulk. I got to a point in my life where I just wanted to give up on my marriage. But something happened. Suddenly we both began to realise that it was God who brought us together and that we should seek his face and ask him to be at the centre of this marriage. I began to recognise my human frailty as a man and I realised that I needed help to put this marriage back on track.

Through my tears, the abiding presence of Almighty God spoke to my spirit and said "I want to turn you from your human frailty and enable you to step into the plan and destiny I have for your life and the life of your family". I then realised that the kind of man that I was needed to change into the man that God wanted me to be. It was at this point that God began to do a work in me that completely transformed my life and it was though this that *Ministry to Men* (MTM) was birthed in my spirit.

I want every man to know that God is still working in my life and through my obedience to him I am constantly seeing that God's purposes and plans for my life are greater than my frustrations; they are more wonderful than my hopes.

Now glory be to God, who by his mighty power at work within us is able to do far more than we would ever dare to ask or even dream of—infinitely beyond our highest prayers, desires, thoughts, or hopes. (Ephesians 3:20 TLB)

His grace is much greater than our difficulties.

And he said unto me, my grace is sufficient for thee: for my strength is made perfect in weakness. Most gladly therefore will I rather glory

> *in my infirmities, that the power of Christ may rest upon me. (2 Corinthians 12:9)."*

His love is sufficient to sustain me in every trial. I trust him because I know that he will never let me down. God is continually at work in my life for he knew me before I came into being.

> *But with your own eyes you saw my body being formed. Even before I was born, you had written in your book everything I would do. (Psalm 139:16 CEV).*

I would like to thank God, who has changed my life dramatically and set me on the road to becoming a man in the true sense of the word. Although I am still on this journey I have seen tremendous transformation in my life each day I awake. Thank you God for caring so much for me.

I would also like to say thank you to my beautiful wife, Maureen, who is not only my wife but also a true friend. She has been patient with me; she supports me, encourages me and always assures me of her love. I want to thank her for her tireless efforts in editing this book. I am blessed to have her as my wife.

To my daughter Michaela who does not realise the impact she has on my life I want to say "I love you". You have brought out a side of me that I will cherish forever.

My Father in heaven, I thank you with all of my heart.

PREFACE

The ability to understand who you really are and what your role is in life does not rest on your intellectual ability. Neither does it rest on logic or reason. It comes from a source that is way above our human understanding. Tapping into that source or connecting to that source will bring you to a point where you will be able to identify who you really are and what you are really capable of achieving. The source that I am referring to is God himself. This same God who made man as a full representation of himself, breathed into him the breath of life and instructed him to go forth and multiply and replenish the earth. In other words the earth was to be filled with the goodness of God because all that God is was poured into man. For we know where the presence of God is there is fullness of joy. Sadly today the world with all its knowledge believes it can accomplish all things without the help of God. Suddenly the world wants to take the goodness of God out of the equation. Man now wants to live independently of God.

So many surveys are done concerning problems in our society and communities. Drug pushing and drug taking is increasing day by day. Domestic violence is increasing day by day. Child abuse is increasing day by day. Absentee fathers are increasing day by day. Robberies, muggings, gang warfare etc the list is endless. Questions are being asked about how to deal with the decline in morality in our nation. Money is continually pumped into the problem. Workshops are set up by local boroughs to try to change the statistics. Man is doing everything he can in his human capacity to create a more stable community, but what about the heart of man? No amount of money can change the heart. Only God by his grace through the Lord Jesus Christ can change a man on the inside. For what we truly are on the inside reflects in our daily actions. No nation, no society, no community will ever change unless man changes on the inside and focuses his attention on the God of heaven. Every man needs Jesus Christ as his Lord and Saviour. Accepting him in your life will cause you to function correctly in all aspects of life. I dare you to be that man.

It is time for us to make a difference in our sphere of influence. Our world needs to get back to its roots where God can manifest his glory and man can replenish the earth with the goodness of God. Every man needs to cry out before God, and seek him like never before. Don't let Christianity be driven out of our schools, our colleges, our homes, or our communities. Don't let governments turn the world away from God. If we take God out of the equation the world will decline and spiral out of control. We need to get back on track. Let every man begin to pray to God the Father for the Holy Sprit to sweep this land. I dare you to be that man.

- If you want to see stronger and healthier marriages, then pray to God the Father, the originator of man and He will direct your path. *I dare you to be that man.*

- If you want to see a safer and more productive community, then pray that God will show you how this can be made possible. *I dare you to be that man.*

- Do you want to be the right kind of man, father or husband? Then pray that you will be a reflection of our heavenly Father. *I dare you to be that man.*

When a man changes on the inside, the world changes also. Every man will function in his role accurately and with wisdom and understanding when he recognizes who he is in Christ Jesus. This book sets out to put men on the right track to authentic manhood. Applying the truths throughout this book will enable you to make the right kind of impact in the nation, the home, the community, and the church. This book is by no means exhaustive, but it will point you in the right direction towards godly manhood.

"Be that man," challenges every man who wants to impact their home, community and nation with good things. It challenges men to turn their hearts to the Father above, asking for wisdom, direction and guidance. Because,

"Every good gift and every perfect gift is from above, and cometh down from the Father of lights, with whom is no variableness, neither shadow of turning". (James 1:17)

Illuminate My Soul

My God illuminate my soul.
When I am broken, make me whole.
Please shine on me your searching rays
That cause me to walk within your ways.

My God illuminate my path
That I may tread the golden way.
Then with each step that's onward trod
Will lead me nearer to thee my God

My God, illuminate my heart
Then humbly I will play my part.
Your light to shine in me so bright
Reflecting your beauty, your presence, your light.

© *R. C. Francis*
(used by permission)

Jesus said, *"I am the light of the world: he that followeth me shall not walk in darkness, but shall have the light of life." (John 8:12)*

CHAPTER 1

GOD'S CREATIVE ACT

[26]And God said, Let us make man in our image, after our likeness: and let them have dominion over the fish of the sea, and over the fowl of the air, and over the cattle, and over all the earth, and over every creeping thing that creepeth upon the earth. [27]So God created man in his own image, in the image of God created he him; male and female created he them. [28]And God blessed them, and God said unto them, Be fruitful, and multiply, and replenish the earth, and subdue it: and have dominion over the fish of the sea, and over the fowl of the air, and over every living thing that moveth upon the earth. (Genesis 1:26-28)

Man is a product of God's creative act. We are made to function as channels of his divine power. We were made to function in an orderly manner. We were made by a blessed God, who blessed us to bless others. In order for man to live a prosperous and blessed life and make an impact in his community and family, he must function with complete obedience to the product maker, which is God himself. God made man in his own image. No other creature, not even the angels were spoken of in the same way. The basic definition of the word "image" is *shadow, representation or likeness.* Therefore the image of God in man reveals God's perspective of mans worth as a representation or shadow of himself in the created world. With that image comes dominion. Notice that God fashioned the nature of man in such a way, that his own image would clearly be on display in man's attitudes, thoughts and actions. This reveals his own nature in the life of the man. It is therefore important for man to understand that a right relationship with God forms the basis for maintaining godly manhood, and that this relationship depends upon a yielded heart followed by a lifestyle of seeking to please God. Many men are frightened of the word "relationship", but our commitment to become the men that God intended from the beginning of time will determine the impact we will make in our families, and communities, because a community is only as good as the people in it.

Good deeds from a good heart

> ^{1}Now the serpent was more subtil than any beast of the field which the LORD God had made. And he said unto the woman, Yea, hath God said, Ye shall not eat of every tree of the garden? ^{2}And the woman said unto the serpent, We may eat of the fruit of the trees of the garden: ^{3}But of the fruit of the tree which is in the midst of the garden, God hath said, Ye shall not eat of it, neither shall ye touch it, lest ye die. ^{4}And the serpent said unto the woman, Ye shall not surely die: ^{5}For God doth know that in the day ye eat thereof, then your eyes shall be opened, and ye shall be as gods, knowing good and evil. (Genesis 3:1-5)

The aim of Satan is to change man's condition. This in turn will affect the society wherein man lives. Satan knows that if he changes the focus of man then he will change society also. The changes that take place in a man will affect the condition of society both now and in the future. In other words, it will affect his generation and the generations to come. The world's perception of manhood needs to be refocused. Our young men must be taught principles that will affect the community in a good way. Our concept of manhood must derive its identity from God's holy word. We are made in God's image and likeness. Therefore as men we need to fulfill our appointed role within the parameters of God's kingdom principles, then our families, society and the community will see clearly on display the very nature of God in and through our lives. The moral decline in society today can change for the better when men accept and carry out their responsibilities with godly motives and methods. It is time to get back to the place where God himself intervenes to bless the work of our hands. Yes, we can make a difference!

When a man abdicates his appointed role within the kingdom of God, it will not only adversely affect the way he relates to his family but society at large will also suffer because of this. In Genesis 1:28 God said to Adam,

> "Be fruitful, and multiply, and replenish the earth, and subdue it: and have dominion over the fish of the sea, and over the fowl of the air, and over every living thing that moveth upon the earth".

Adam at this point is in a wonderful relationship with God. The Father who blesses him with good things carefully watches over him. As long as Adam maintained that relationship through personal acts of obedience by living according to the spoken word of God, he would then be able to be fruitful and multiply and replenish the earth with a people whose heart is governed and directed by the presence and power of God.

God willed that the man he created in his image should be his chosen vessel to build a home, a community and a nation that is pleasing to him.

In order to lead man to full moral and spiritual development, God gave him specific commands and specific prohibitions to govern his behaviour. That same behaviour needs to be passed on to the young men of the future *(Be fruitful and multiply...)*. God also gave man the power of choice and set before him the privilege of growing in divine favour. The moral decline in the society we live can change for the better, when man begins to yield himself and allows God to operate in his heart.

> *⁵A good man produces good deeds from a good heart. And an evil man produces evil deeds from his hidden wickedness. Whatever is in the heart overflows into speech. (*Luke 6:45 TLB)

As we live in an intimate relationship with God, his spirit will energize our hearts and enable us to produce the fruit of righteousness that will bring peace and harmony to both the individual and society. If we choose to remain in our sinful nature *(a life that seeks to please itself, a life that chooses to get along without God)*, then we will continue to harm humanity and bring dissension and harm to our society, communities and families, with devastating results. The greatest change that needs to happen in our world today is for every man to turn his heart back to God and begin to function in his image and likeness. When man changes inwardly, society will change also. What we pass on or what we leave behind determines the destiny of the generations to come.

To ensure that a boy becomes the kind of man that will positively affect his community, we as fathers need to examine our lives to determine whether we have made any impact in our families, communities and society at large, and whether we have learned from our mistakes and failures. If men cannot acknowledge to their sons that they have made mistakes and that they have failed in some part of their lives, then a boy will grow up never knowing how to deal with everyday situations. Failure is a teacher. If we cannot learn when we have failed then we will not accomplish much in life. Understand this, we have all failed at some point in our lives. Many of us have made mistakes. But it is what you do about it that counts. Having a heart that is willing to function under the guidance of God the Father through humble obedience to him will point you on the right road for right living.

The psalmist, David, was a man who turned his heart to the Father through humble obedience. David made mistakes. He was in his palace one day and looked over and saw Bathsheba taking a bath. He began to lust after her, they began an affair and she became pregnant. In order to try and cover up their affair David had her husband Uriah brought back from battle to Jerusalem hoping that it would look like Uriah, and not David, had impregnated Bathsheba. But being a loyal soldier whose troops were dying in battle, Uriah did not feel comfortable having pleasure with his wife while his men were dying. David became frustrated so he had Uriah put in the heat of the battle which he knew was the fiercest, and Uriah was killed. This was a deliberate act to cover his sin. David, after being confronted by Nathan the prophet, acknowledged his sin and he began to cry out to God.

> *O loving and kind God, have mercy. Have pity upon me and take away the awful stain of my transgressions. [2]Oh, wash me, cleanse me from this guilt. Let me be pure again. [3]For I admit my shameful deed—it haunts me day and night. [4]It is against you and you alone I sinned and did this terrible thing. You saw it all, and your sentence against me is just. [5]But I was born a sinner, yes, from the moment my mother conceived me. [6]You deserve honesty from the heart; yes, utter sincerity and truthfulness. Oh, give me this wisdom. [7]Sprinkle me with the cleansing blood and I shall be clean again. Wash me and I shall be whiter than snow. [8]And after you have punished me, give me back my joy again. [9]Don't keep looking at my sins—erase them from your sight. [10]Create in me a new, clean heart, O God, filled with clean thoughts and right desires. [11]Don't toss me aside, banished forever from your presence. Don't take your Holy Spirit from me. [12]Restore to me again the joy of your salvation, and make me willing to obey you. [13]Then I will teach your ways to other sinners, and they—guilty like me—will repent and return to you. (Psalm 51:1-13 TLB)*

David had valued his relationship with God. He had known what it meant to be in the presence of God. He knew how important it was to be in the image of God. His cry came from a heart, which needed renewal. David cried out to the Lord not only to be renewed but that he might continue to be maintained in the divine presence by God's spirit.

David had learned to subject himself to the will of God, and as a result his seed was blessed throughout the generations to come. He had made great impact throughout his rule. The nation had changed because of his godly leadership. But more importantly, he was able to pass on a powerful legacy to his son, Solomon. This legacy was not about gold or silver. This legacy was the blessings of God. David was on his deathbed when he instructed Solomon to ensure that he walks in God's ways as he himself had done, and through obedience he would prosper.

> *[1]Now the days of David drew nigh that he should die; and he charged Solomon his son, saying, [2]I go the way of all the earth:* <u>be thou strong therefore, and shew thyself a man</u> *(emphasis mine); [3]And keep the charge of the LORD thy God, to walk in his ways, to keep his statutes, and his commandments, and his judgments, and his testimonies, as it is written in the law of Moses, that thou mayest prosper in all that thou doest, and whithersoever thou turnest thyself: [4]That the LORD may continue his word which he spake concerning me, saying, If thy children take heed to their way, to walk before me in truth with all their heart and with all their soul, there shall not fail thee (said he) a man on the throne of Israel.* (1 Kings 2:1-4)

David stressed to Solomon the need to make God and his laws the very centre of his life. The fact is, it was important for Solomon to understand that in order to be a man and in order to function effectively as a man, he needed to continually seek the originator of man and that was God himself. And he needed to ensure that he applied God's word to his life.

Every community, society, and nation needs men who are in right standing with God; men of integrity, influence and intimacy.

Men of integrity are those who will keep their word and will not waver. They are honest and sound. These same men will apply biblical principles to their lives, work, home and community. I dare you to be that man.

Men of influence are those who will make a difference in their home, business, community and church. Influencing other men to move out of their present condition and stand up for the word of God and allow the word to affect their lives dramatically. I dare you to be that man.

Men of intimacy are those, if they are married, whose top priority is to cultivate healthy relationships with his wife and children, or healthy relationships with others in his sphere of influence. I dare you to be that man.

Intimacy is not about sleeping around. It is not about smooth talking women into bed outside of marriage. Your intentions should always be honourable and your determined purpose as men should be to have a deep and personal relationship with God through Jesus Christ, for it is through this relationship that the true value of intimacy will be evidenced in your life.

David, on his deathbed, felt it was necessary to pass on wise counsel to Solomon his son. Solomon assumed leadership of Israel at the age of twenty. It was apparent that he needed something far greater than his natural instincts to be able to govern the people of God. Solomon had a need. He needed to be able to show himself a man as David his father had instructed. He was twenty years old and would have to take on the very large task of leading the people of God after the demise of his father. Perhaps he felt his own immaturity. But the voice of his father David rang in his ears: - *"Be strong, show thyself a man, follow God's instructions and you shall prosper"*.

While Solomon took heed to his father's advice, the Lord God appeared to him in a dream and said, *"Ask what I shall give thee"*. Solomon wanted an understanding heart, a hearing heart, a heart that was inclined to do the will of God. He wanted to be able to lead and govern with integrity, trust and truth. Our commitment should be to please God in all aspects of our lives and determine from him the way that we should go. To bring about the right kind of change in our families, communities and society we must first be determined to become men who live and move in the image and likeness of God. Solomon took heed to his father's advice and because of this, his way was prosperous.

> Father, give me a heart that is inclined to do your will

CHAPTER 2

REFLECTING THE HEAVENLY FATHER

> *⁵And thou shalt love the LORD thy God with all thine heart, and with all thy soul, and with all thy might. ⁶And these words, which I command thee this day, shall be in thine heart: ⁷And thou shalt teach them diligently unto thy children, and shalt talk of them when thou sittest in thine house, and when thou walkest by the way, and when thou liest down, and when thou risest up. ⁸And thou shalt bind them for a sign upon thine hand, and they shall be as frontlets between thine eyes. ⁹And thou shalt write them upon the posts of thy house, and on thy gates. (Deuteronomy 6:5-9)*

The intent of this passage is that the Word of God should be hidden in our hearts and should constantly be a source of devotion and obedience to the Lord. The main thrust is that we should teach our children the Word of God. Those that are well taught in word and truth will prosper in every area of their lives if they act on what they have learnt. Those that love the Lord God themselves should do what they can to ensure their children engage in the same love, which will bring the grace of God upon their lives. That good thing which is committed to us from God the Father we must carefully transmit to those that come after us, that it may be perpetuated.

Throughout our lives as fathers we must make a deeper commitment to exemplify Jesus Christ in and through our lives, so that our children develop a correct perspective both intellectually and emotionally of our heavenly Father. As our children grow we tell them about God being a heavenly Father, and as they continue to grow they begin to develop certain ideas about God. Because of various kinds of experiences the child has with their parents particularly their fathers, a picture of God begins to form in their minds as they watch the way their father's react to life's situations on a daily basis. If father is kind and loving then so is God. If a father is cold and cruel then so is God. Therefore it is important that we emulate God in and through our lives and become a reflection of our heavenly Father.

The Apostle Paul made it clear in his letters to Timothy that a mark of maturity in a man is the way he functions as a father. His children particularly will reflect how well he has fulfilled this God ordained role.

He must rule his own household well, keeping his children under control with true dignity, commanding their respect in every way and keeping them respectful. For if a man does not know how to rule his own household, how is he to take care of the church of God? (1 Timothy 3:4-5 TAB)

Having a well-ordered household should be the goal of every Christian man.

Our duty as husbands

[25]Husbands, love your wives, even as Christ also loved the church, and gave himself for it. (Ephesians 5:25)

[7]You husbands must be careful of your wives, being thoughtful of their needs and honoring them as the weaker sex. Remember that you and your wife are partners in receiving God's blessings, and if you don't treat her as you should, your prayers will not get ready answers. (1 Peter 3:7 TLB)

Our duty as fathers

*[4]And, ye fathers, provoke not your children to wrath: but bring them up in the nurture and admonition of the Lord. (*Ephesians 6:4*)*

*[6]Teach a child to choose the right path, and when he is older, he will remain upon it. (*Proverbs 22:6 TLB*)*

Your relationship to your wife should be as important to you as breathing. Relationships matter to God and that is why he ordained marriage. We reflect God in our lives when we truly love, honour and respect our wives and become sensitive to their needs.

We reflect God in our lives by ensuring that our children from an early age are trained up and taught right from wrong and given clear instruction on the path he or she should take. God is reflected in that training when we choose his way and not our own. We are to: -

> Focus *upward* - to receive God's word and clear direction.
>
> Focus *inward* - by allowing God's word, divine favour and power to permeate every fibre of our being.
>
> Focus *outward* - by putting God's word into action, activating God's authority in our lives for this is our right as obedient children of God.

We represent God by receiving and implanting his word into the lives of our family. Our lives become a reflection of the heavenly Father. We speak the things he speaks. We love the way he loves. We represent God through teaching and instructing our family in the ways and word of God. We have the responsibility to govern our families on behalf of God. In 1 Timothy 3: 4-5 TAB we read: -

> *He must rule his own household well, keeping his children under control with true dignity, commanding their respect in every way and keeping them respectful. For if a man does not know how to rule his own household, how is he to take care of the church of God?*

Rule means to stand out in front of or to stand at the head of. We put ourselves between our family and the pressures and dangers of life. We also go in front of them and set an example of godly living.

We go in front of our family and set an example of godly living

---

Encounter

Lord, as I seek a closer walk with thee
Hear and answer me
As I humbly bow the knee before your presence
Breathe your Holy Spirit in me

For I am nothing of myself, my life is not my own
Just one encounter with you Lord, and I'll be yours alone

Onward, forward, I would go, I'll walk in victory
I'll walk in victory by your grace
Which you bestow on me

Lord, as I seek a closer walk with thee
Hear and answer me

© *R.C. Francis*
(used by permission)

CHAPTER 3

TAKE YOUR PLACE AS HEAD OF YOUR FAMILY AND TRUST GOD FOR THE GRACE YOU NEED

If you make up your mind to be the kind of father and husband God is looking for, you must be willing to open up your whole heart and life to him. As you allow him to expose all sin and do his purging work in you, you will move out of the twilight zone and into the clear sunlight of God's favour. There you will begin to understand all that is involved in being a father.

Let us therefore come boldly unto the throne of grace that we may obtain mercy and find grace to help in time of need. (Hebrews 4:16)

In all our approaches to this throne of grace for mercy, we should come with a humble heart to express freely and boldly with complete liberty of spirit and a readiness of free speech. We should ask in faith, nothing wavering or doubting. We should come with a spirit of adoption, as children whose desire is to be reconciled to God the Father. We are indeed to come with complete reverence and godly fear, not with terror and amazement, not as if we were dragged through the streets but kindly invited to the mercy seat where grace and favor reigns, and loves to exert and exalt itself towards us. The office that Jesus occupies as high priest should be the basis of our approach to the throne of grace. We have boldness to enter into the holiest by the blood of Jesus. He is our advocate. He will plead to the Father on our behalf and the Father will respond with grace and mercy.

Addressing God as our Father

"And lead us not into temptation but deliver us from evil". (Matthew 6:13a)

When a man chooses to live for God and follow God's way, the devil is not pleased. At certain times throughout our Christian walk, temptation rears its ugly head stronger and more vociferous than ever before. It is at this point that we, as men, must have a greater trust in the Lord our God. Self must decrease so that Christ can increase. This will give us greater power to deal with the pressures that we face daily in our lives. Our hearts should be as the Father's heart. Our eyes should see what the Father sees. The full demonstration and manifestation of being a godly man of God, formed in his character shaped in his likeness, walking in his power, living in victory, can only become activated or fully operational when we begin to see God as Our Father and yield ourselves in obedience to him.

> *" Humble yourselves-feeling very insignificant-in the presence of the Lord, and He will exalt you-He will lift you up and make your lives significant".* (James 4:10 TAB)

When we are under pressure it is important to understand that our God has not permitted the situation to trap us, but as we remain close to him we will find his way of escape, and our godly response to temptation will demonstrate the authenticity of our faith.

> [12]*Happy is the man who doesn't give in and do wrong when he is tempted, for afterwards he will get as his reward the crown of life that God has promised those who love him.* [13]*And remember, when someone wants to do wrong it is never God who is tempting him, for God never wants to do wrong and never tempts anyone else to do it.* [14]*Temptation is the pull of man's own evil thoughts and wishes.* [15]*These evil thoughts lead to evil actions and afterwards to the death penalty from God.* [16]*So don't be misled, dear brothers.* [17]*But whatever is good and perfect comes to us from God, the Creator of all light, and he shines forever without change or shadow.* (James 1:12-17 TLB).

Jesus Christ himself trusted God the Father fully. As he yielded himself, he clearly demonstrated the wholesome relationship that he has with the Father, one that we can emulate.

> *"For because He Himself - in His humanity - has suffered in being tempted, tested, and tried - He is able - immediately to run to the cry of - assist and relieve - those who are being tempted and tested and tried and who therefore are being exposed to suffering. (Hebrews 2:18 TAB)*

> [4]*For God did not spare even the angels who sinned, but threw them into hell, chained in gloomy caves and darkness until the judgment day.* [5]*And he did not spare any of the people who lived in ancient times before the flood except Noah, the one man who spoke up for God, and his family of seven. At that time God completely destroyed the whole*

world of ungodly men with the vast flood. ⁶Later, he turned the cities of Sodom and Gomorrah into heaps of ashes and blotted them off the face of the earth, making them an example for all the ungodly in the future to look back upon and fear. ⁷⁻⁸But at the same time the Lord rescued Lot out of Sodom because he was a good man, sick of the terrible wickedness he saw everywhere around him day after day. ⁹So also the Lord can rescue you and me from the temptations that surround us, and continue to punish the ungodly until the day of final judgment comes. (1 Peter 2:7-9 TLB)

God can rescue us from the temptations that surround us

⁹After this manner therefore pray ye: Our Father which art in heaven, Hallowed be thy name. ¹⁰Thy kingdom come. Thy will be done in earth, as it is in heaven. ¹¹Give us this day our daily bread. ¹²And forgive us our debts, as we forgive our debtors. ¹³And lead us not into temptation, but deliver us from evil: For thine is the kingdom, and the power, and the glory, for ever. Amen. (Matthew 6:9-13)

Jesus in this chapter continues to warn the disciples against the corrupt practices of the Pharisees.

⁵And when thou prayest, thou shalt not be as the hypocrites are: for they love to pray standing in the synagogues and in the corners of the streets, that they may be seen of men. Verily I say unto you, they have their reward. ⁶But thou, when thou prayest, enter into thy closet, and when thou hast shut thy door, pray to thy Father which is in secret; and thy Father which seeth in secret shall reward thee openly. ⁷But when ye pray, use not vain repetitions, as the heathen do: for they think that they shall be heard for their much speaking. ⁸Be not ye therefore like unto them: for your Father knoweth what things ye have need of, before ye ask him. (Matthew 6:5-8*)*

Jesus then gives clear instruction and directs the disciples to do better. Because we do not know what to pray for as we ought, Jesus helps our infirmities by putting words into our mouths. *Matthew 6:9a. "After this manner therefore pray ye".*

So much corruption had crept into the duty of prayer among the scribes and Pharisees that the Lord Jesus Christ saw it was necessary to give a new direction for prayer. He wanted to show the disciples a method of prayer that would deepen their dependence on the one who is the Father of all; a prayer, which does not seek the praise of men but the power and presence of God himself.

Jesus composed this prayer at the request of his disciples. It is instructive and concise - a letter sent from earth to heaven: -

          F.A.O.   ....God the Father
          Address.   ....Heaven
          Contents...............Requests
          Close....................For thine is
          Seal......................Amen

Here we are taught how to address ourselves to God and what title to give him. It also indicates that we must pray not only for ourselves, but also with and for others, because we are members one of another and we are called into fellowship with each other. We must clearly address him as ***"our father"***. This shows that we know him as our creator and we know him as the father to all mankind. We must focus on him in prayer and our thoughts of him must be pure. As ***"our father"*** he will deny us nothing that is good for us. In this way the intimate father-child relationship between God and man is clearly emphasized.

CHAPTER 4

SPIRITUAL MATURITY IN THE FAMILY AND HOME

Jesus replied "The Son can do nothing by himself, he does only what he sees the Father doing, and in the same way. (John 5:19 TLB)

There is a perfect correspondence and harmony between the Father and the Son. The Son does not oppose the Father, nor does the Father oppose the Son. Jesus does what God does. There is a personal and intimate relationship between the Father and the Son.

It is therefore important that we as men build our lives around this very word of Scripture.

"The Son can do nothing by himself, he does only what he sees the Father doing, and in the same way".

1) We must be found *doing* the will of the Father (for it is in doing we become).

2) The Son conforms to the Father (we fashion ourselves after our heavenly Father).

3) Christ himself was so devoted to his Father's will that it was impossible for him to act independently of him. Whatever the Father did the Son kept it ever in his view.

4) As fathers we need to comprehend that we should not seek to act independently of God, but we must acknowledge that ultimately fatherhood begins with God, and that behind all of life is the fatherhood of God.

"For this cause I bow the knees unto the Father of our Lord Jesus Christ. Of whom all the family in heaven and earth is named ". (Ephesians 3:14-15)

5) As fathers we need to prepare the soil of our hearts through prayer, study, and communion, to enable a constant flow of the power of God to clearly govern our lives. Our ultimate aim is to become a reflection of our heavenly Father.

6) There must be a deep longing in the soul for more of God's presence and power, more of His truth and grace. Change will come when the people of God allow themselves to be prepared through the discipline of fervent prayer.

"The effectual fervent prayer of a righteous man availeth much. (James 5:16)

7) Our knowledge of Jesus Christ, our relationship with him, our union with him through prayer, is the source, the very foundation of our strength. It is through this relationship that we need to cry out to the Father to enable us to have a deeper commitment to serve as examples, or become an official copy of the Lord Jesus Christ in all areas of our lives. This will enable our children to develop a correct perspective both intellectually and emotionally of our heavenly Father. As stated in the earlier part of this book, our children, as they are growing up, begin to develop certain ideas about God. We must ensure that we watch the way we react to everyday life. Therefore it is of vital importance that we emulate God in and through our lives, and become a reflection of our heavenly Daddy. This will enable us to understand our role as biblical fathers.

But I want you to know and realize that Christ is the head of every man, the head of the women is her husband, and the head of Christ is God. (1 Corinthians 11:3 NIV)

This scripture speaks of authority for the sake of order, in order to deal with a specific problem that existed at the time. The important word here is *head*.

"The head of every man is Christ; and the head of the woman is the man; and the head of Christ is God."

The *head* is that portion of the body that gives the direction. This verse does not say that the head of every Christian man is Christ. It says the head of every man is Christ. It is the normal and correct order for Christ to be the head of every man this will ensure that the man is divinely directed to fulfill his role the way that God intended. Until a man is governed by Christ, he is not operating the way God intended. Some men are governed by drink, some are governed by passion, most are governed by the flesh. Every man should be governed by Jesus Christ. This is how we will be able to bring about change in our homes, in our communities and in society as a whole. The greatest thing that can happen to any man is when he steps away from acting independently of God and steps into the arena of God's presence with all humility and cries out to him and says, "Lord I want to do things your way, my way has not worked. I know by doing things your way I can effect change in my sphere of influence". It is here that God will respond giving clear direction, knowing that the man will follow.

As Jesus looks up and speaks to God on our behalf, he then looks down and pours what God says into the spirit of man.

As the man looks up to Jesus Christ and speaks to Him concerning his family, he then looks down and speaks the words of Jesus to his wife and children. As fathers we impart the principles and directives of Jesus Christ into the lives of our children.

FATHERHOOD IS FOR LIFE AND IS A VITAL MINISTRY

CHAPTER 5

LIVING UNDER AN OPEN HEAVEN IN YOUR HOME

God desires the dwelling place of every man to be a fertile and fruitful garden where the awesomeness of his Spirit reigns and men are free to speak of his word, his anointing, his grace and truth therein. He desires that the home of every man be filled with a blessed, rich, ambience of love and acceptance, where words of divine revelation knowledge fall frequently from our lips.

Whenever the Holy Spirit is welcomed into our home he makes the word of God come alive in the heart, burning its truth deep into man's spirit. He comes over us with divine creativity and direction, ordering our steps for the day ahead. For this is the kind of house God finds great joy to be in. God clearly wants to revive our spirit and give us strength and resolve to rise up and rid our homes of the unclean things that vex them.

Behold I give unto you power (The right to command*) serpents and scorpions, and over all the power of the enemy. And nothing shall by any means hurt you.* (Luke 10:19) *(Author's definition in brackets).*

God desires that the Holy Spirit permeate our homes giving us the will to get and keep our house in order. The Holy Spirit should be the prime mover of inspiration in the life of every man. Every man will have serious problems in his house if happiness, joy and love, are absent. Whatever measure of love, joy, peace and commitment you see in the faces of your wife and children is the same measure of freedom the Holy Ghost enjoys in your house.

Fathers it is time to purge our houses so that the windows of heaven can be open over our dwelling place. Where the presence of God is there is wonderful liberty. Our home is well guarded when the man of that home does his job as the priest by interceding for his family on a regular basis, thanking God for his family each day and ensuring that he speaks a blessing upon the lives of all the family invoking the name of Jesus upon them. It is these actions that enable the home to be a place of peace, love, joy, and security. I pray that every man will speak good things into the atmosphere and the windows of heaven will be open over their lives and the lives of your family members, eternally.

We need to remember that as husbands our position as the head of the home does not make us superior to the woman. Just as God the Father, Jesus Christ the Son, and the Holy Spirit are all one but with distinct functions and characteristics, so husbands and wives are one with differing functions and characteristics. A man and his wife are to be one in every way. They simply have differing roles and responsibilities in the home.

> *And Adam said this is now bone of my bones and flesh of my flesh: she shall be called women because she was taken out of man. Therefore shall a man leave his father and his mother and shall cleave unto his wife, and they shall be one flesh.* (Genesis 2:23)

A woman is not inferior to her husband. Her role and position are not of any lesser value or importance. Men and women fulfil different roles. The biblical pattern of placing a wife under the authority of her husband is God's plan for protecting her and the home.

> *Submitting, yourselves one to another in the fear of God. Wives submit yourselves unto your own husbands, as unto the Lord. For the husband is the head of the wife, even as Christ is the head of the church: and He is the Saviour of the body. Therefore as the church is subject unto Christ, so let the wives be to their own husbands in everything. Husbands love your wives, even as Christ also loved the church, and gave Himself for it.* (Ephesians 5:21-25)

Jesus carefully maintained a right relationship with his father. He wanted to meet the Father's approval in everything he did. This was a priority for Jesus because the power and authority to fulfil his mission were directly linked to his purpose. A man and a woman united in a marriage relationship need the same unity of purpose, mind and spirit. When this unity is missing both husband and wife are open to the guiles of Satan.

"Submitting yourselves one to another in the fear of God." (Ephesians 5:21a). This means that you do not try to run the church. Pastors, officers in the church and members of the church, are all to submit to one another in the fear of God. No one should say, " I'll do as I please regardless of what anyone else thinks or feels." Such an attitude is not a mark of a spirit-filled believer. Submitting to one another in the

fear of God is another mark of being spirit-filled. Therefore, out of respect for Jesus Christ, let us have due regard for one another.

Submit is a very mild word. It is a loving word. The way we respond to the Lord is that we love him because he first loved us. A very personal, loving relationship is the ground for submission. Paul is definitely speaking to believers about Christian marriage. Wives, *understand and support* your husbands in ways that will honour Christ.

The husband provides leadership to his wife the way Christ does to His church, not by domineering but by *cherishing*. So just as the church submits to Christ as he exercises leadership, wives should likewise submit (respond) to their husbands.

Husbands go all out and give a hundred per cent of your love to your wives, exactly as Jesus Christ did for the church. This love is marked by *giving*, not by *getting*. Christ's love makes the church whole. Everything he says and does is designed to bring the best out of her; dressing her in stunning white silk, glowing with holiness. Husbands likewise need to respond to the needs of their wives, treat them well and bring out the best in them. I dare you to be that man!

As men we need to be aware of the atmosphere created by the words that we permit to be spoken in our homes.

"The words that I speak unto you they are spirit, and they are life. (John 6:63b)

Let the words of my mouth, and the meditation of my heart, be acceptable in thy sight, O Lord, my strength and my redeemer. (Psalm 19:14)

We need to remember that our mouths are continually releasing blessings or curses into our environments. As men (husbands and fathers) we have the authority to speak blessings into our households. Fathers in the Old Testament were in the "blessing business". In fact, a father's blessing was so important, that it was considered the most valuable part of a son's inheritance. As was mentioned earlier, we need to speak good things into the atmosphere. There must be an environment where fellowship becomes a way of life; where communities can dwell together in peace; where families begin to understand the true meaning of care and support. Our impact into the lives of others is vital as it determines how the next generation will respond to the challenges of the future. Remember we are made in God's image after his likeness. We are a full representation of all that God is. When we truly grasp this truth it will enable us to effect change in a powerful way. When we speak it will be as though God spoke. Now is the time for every man to humble himself before God. It is time to make a difference. Let us bring God back to our nations, our communities and our families. I dare you to be that man!

We men need to restore God's order in our homes and our communities. This will require us to work our way back, undoing each step that led to our demise. Having order in our lives is important to God. Sometimes we pay more attention to everybody else except God. Our world needs real men; men who are living and moving in the presence of God; men who desire to be channels of the power of God. Men who will dare to stand on the authority of God's word and apply the truths therein to their lives. I dare you to be that man!

SOMETIMES WE PAY MORE ATTENTION TO EVERYONE ELSE EXCEPT GOD

The heavens are open to those fathers who carefully assess the condition of their homes and communities and take the necessary steps to establish holiness and freedom.

Blessed is everyone that feareth the Lord; that walketh in His way. For thou shalt eat the labour of thine hands; happy shalt thou be; and it shall be well with thee. Thy wife shall be a fruitful vine by the sides of thy house thy children like olive plants round about thy table. Behold that thus shall the man be blessed that feareth the Lord. (Psalm 128:1-4)

My friend, you can never have a happy home until the fear of the Lord is in that home, until the members of the family walk day by day in the ways of the Lord.

You cannot get away from the fact that, unless there is a reverential fear of God and obedience to him, there will not be a happy home. Children need to know that if their parents love the Lord, serve and obey him, there is no substitute for the godly life. You can go to all of the conferences you want to, but you will never have a happy home until your relationship with God is right. Every person must develop a personal relationship with Jesus Christ. It is through this relationship that God will speak and give clear direction throughout your life.

CHAPTER 6

JESUS THE PATTERN FOR AUTHENTIC MANHOOD

There is an urgent need for men everywhere to emulate Jesus Christ, to accept the call of God in his life and take full responsibility for the moral and spiritual leadership of the community, the home, the nations and the church. It is therefore important for every man to pattern himself after Jesus Christ who was clearly a genuine man in all areas of his life. He clearly knew what it meant to be in God's image, after his likeness. Jesus became all that God wanted him to be. It is in the same way that we are to become all that God wants us to be. Genuine manhood can only be found in the person of Jesus Christ. Establishing this relationship will enable every man to approach every day knowing that he is qualified to be a genuine man. This means that every man will know how to live as a man, how to act as a man and his attitude will glorify God. It will be through this change that God himself will pour his power into man and through this outpouring he will heal society; he will teach him how to lead his family and the nation will develop better, trustworthy and healthy relationships. This is significant to bring about change in our world.

Jesus The Pattern For Mentoring

Just how does a boy become a man - not just any man, but a man who has a hunger and a thirst to follow after God? What is man? What process produces a man? How do you know when you have become a genuine man? These questions are critical to all of life.

As fathers, we need to find the trail back to the bible. The bible provides a complete guide to developing as godly men with high standards of morality and righteousness. If you were to ask most young men today, "how does a man act?" or "what are men's unique responsibilities?" or "what role should a man assume in marriage?" they would have no idea of how to answer these questions.

Some are asking these very questions right now. In fact many of the social problems of our day (plummeting morality, rising crime, violence, abuse, reckless, pleasure seeking) spring from the soil of directionless, disconnected sons.

Many men today are searching again for their true masculine identity. Fathers today are beginning to ask, "How can I raise my boy into a man - a genuine man?" Our sons need something more from us than just love and support; they need help in becoming genuine men. We must raise our sons with moral & spiritual vision. We must increase their desire for spiritual discovery and growth. Young men need fathers, grandfathers and uncles to be involved in their lives. They need people who will love them, teach them and discipline them. Every young boy needs to be taught good principles and values that will produce a society that is productive in good things. These principles and values must be based on the truth of God's word. Our young men must be mentored in the ways of righteousness and moral standing. Those of us men who have laboured for Jesus Christ, have found that through him we can deal wisely with our problems. We must now push that energy into becoming mentors of the young. We must not allow these truths to follow us to the grave; but we must invest these truths into the lives of our young men as Jesus did to the disciples. Our young men need to know what genuine manhood is. But they will not know unless we teach them in word and in deed. Every son deserves a father who will fill his life with love, affirmation, and blessing. Every son needs vision, direction and solid answers from his father. Questions such as *"What is a man?" "What are man's responsibilities?" "What does a man believe?" "How should a man behave?"* The answer to each of these questions can be found in the Word of God.

Without wise leadership, a nation is in trouble, but with good counsellors there is safety. Proverbs 11:14 TLB

Every young boy needs to be taught good principles and values that will produce a society that is productive in good things

CHAPTER 7

A SPECIAL MESSAGE TO MEN EVERYWHERE

^{12}Now we have received, not the spirit of the world, but the spirit which is of God; that we might know the things that are freely given to us of God. ^{13}Which things also we speak, not in the words which man's wisdom teacheth, but which the Holy Ghost teacheth; comparing spiritual things with spiritual. ^{14}But the natural man receiveth not the things of the Spirit of God: for they are foolishness unto him: neither can he know them, because they are spiritually discerned. (1 Corinthians 2:14)

The word *natural* when used in this passage of scripture is used in accordance with human nature. It means that we are governed by our natural instincts independent of God. The things of God become meaningless to man because man feels he has the capability to function without the help of God. The world is in turmoil because the things of God are no longer important to man and that is why we no longer produce young men who are interested in the things of God. Men of God need to step out of the natural and into the supernatural to be able to effect change and make a significant impact in their sphere of influence. Our governments need to hear from God. Our leaders need to hear from God. In fact, if every man cried out for the Holy Spirit to enter their lives there would be no domestic violence and there would be no absentee fathers. Change will come when men of God everywhere humble themselves in the sight of God. I dare you to be that man!

Change will come when men of God everywhere humble themselves in the sight of God.

---

^{12} But God has given us his Spirit. That's why we don't think the same way that the people of this world think. That's also why we can

recognize the blessings that God has given us.[13] *Every word we speak was taught to us by God's Spirit, not by human wisdom. And this same Spirit helps us teach spiritual things to spiritual people.*[14]*That's why only someone who has God's Spirit can understand spiritual blessings. Anyone who doesn't have God's Spirit thinks these blessings are foolish.* (1 Corinthians 2:14.Contemporary English Version)

Prayer (Your Kind of Man)

Father, give me your Holy Spirit that I can think your thoughts. Teach me to recognise your voice, that I may apply your word in my life. Let me be a channel of your power. Enable me to humble myself before you. I desire to be your kind of man for when I am your kind of man you will make the crooked way straight. Amen

Anyone who ceases to function spiritually is separated from God. This suggests a failure to live as one should and that person will only function in the human condition. The revelations or teachings of God are meaningless to the natural man because in his heart his tendency is to operate independent of God and centre his focus on himself. He does not readily accept or welcome the teachings and revelations of the Spirit of God.

[18]*If the world hate you, ye know that it hated me before it hated you.* [19]*If ye were of the world, the world would love his own: but because ye are not of the world, but I have chosen you out of the world, therefore the world hateth you.* [20]*Remember the word that I said unto you, the servant is not greater than his Lord. If they have persecuted me, they will also persecute you; if they have kept my saying, they will keep yours also.* [21]*But all these things will they do unto you for my name's sake, because they know not him that sent me.* [22]*If I had not come and spoken unto them, they had not had sin: but now they have no cloke for their sin.* [23]*He that hateth me hateth my Father also.* (John 15:18-23)

Those who choose to live independently of God experience the world's love for them. This world that we live in is a system organized by Satan who himself hates and opposes all that is godly. Jesus was reminding us in the above scripture that if we were of the world, the world would love us but because we are not of the world, the world hates us. He also said that the world hated him long before it hated us. It is amazing that when Christians try to bring good to the world, the world ridicules them. Jesus came that the world could have life and have it more abundantly, yet the world crucified him. The message of the gospel is to bring peace to he world yet the world wants peace on its own terms and still there are those that oppose peace. Questions are continually asked about the problems that the world is experiencing. Some even go so far as blaming God for all the problems. But the problem is due to the progression of man. Through his developmental years and the advancement of technology, man has learned to live independently of God, and has attempted to get his needs met apart from him. God has been taken out of the equation.

> *For they that are after the flesh do mind the things of the flesh; but they that are after the Spirit the things of the Spirit. For to be carnally minded is death; but to be spiritually minded is life and peace. Because the carnal mind is enmity against God: for it is not subject to the law of God, neither indeed can be. So then they that are in the flesh cannot please God.* (Romans 8:5-8.)

An unbeliever cares only for his sinful interests and has no regard for God. The unsaved lead lives which are totally void of spiritual life and ability. A believer, then who gives in to his sin nature is acting like the unsaved.

> *For you are still unspiritual, having the nature of the flesh-under the control of ordinary impulses. For as long as there are envying, and jealousy and wrangling and factions among you, are you not unspiritual and of the flesh, behaving yourselves after a human standard and like mere unchanged men?* (1 Corinthians chapter 3:6 TAB)

Those who are living the life of the flesh (*that is independent of God*) catering to the impulse and appetites of their carnal nature (*governed by human nature instead of the spirit of God, attending to the lusts which have their source in man's fallen and corrupt nature*) cannot please or satisfy, God, or be acceptable to him. This means that man has not grown spiritually and lacks spiritual discernment. And this is a consequence of man's relationship to God. Clearly every man needs to grow in grace and in the knowledge of our saviour, Jesus Christ. We have within us the ability to do this, but our desires are weak. It is therefore imperative that every man cries out to God for divine revelation on how to enter into the spirit of the gospel. For it is through this revelation that God will be able to intervene in our lives and cause us to become men of integrity, identity, and influence.

CHAPTER 8

MAKING A DIFFERENCE MEANS YOU MUST BE BORN AGAIN

[17]When someone becomes a Christian, he becomes a brand new person inside. He is not the same anymore. A new life has begun! (2 Corinthians 5:17 TLB)

In the born again experience, the old self dies and the "new man" comes alive. Before we were born again we were separated from God, pleasing ourselves, feeding the appetites of the flesh, and our mindset was completely programmed with thought patterns, habits and ideas, which alienated us from God. Even though when we have accepted Jesus Christ into our lives our flesh still remains in opposition to God and tries to operate independent of him. This is where there is a struggle. The devil knows the weakness of the flesh and unless that flesh is brought under subjection to the will of God, we will go right back from where we came. For many men this struggle has caused many problems. Some deny that they have such a problem others try to deal with it themselves. If we remain independent of God we will fail most miserably. God wants us to draw near to him where we can live a life of total victory. You and I were not designed to function unaided or independent of God.

My child, remember my teachings and instructions and obey them completely. They will help you live a long and prosperous life. Let love and loyalty always show like a necklace, and write them in your mind. God and people will like you and consider you a success. With all your heart you must trust the LORD and not your own judgment. Always let him lead you, and he will clear the road for you to follow. Don't ever think that you are wise enough, but respect the LORD and stay away from evil. (Proverbs chapter 3:1-7 CEV)

When we fully submit and humble ourselves before God, we are inviting him to take the throne in our lives and to occupy what is rightfully his so that we can function the way he intended as people who are spiritually alive in Christ Jesus. Men, whether young or old, are challenged to listen, trust, obey, fear and honour God, being subject to his will. This shows that we have a desire to be directed by the grace and wisdom of God. This inward desire to follow after the instructions of the

Lord will produce great success in our homes, communities, nations and relationships as a whole. All dependence on our own understanding must be relinquished and must be replaced by a total trust and reliance upon God. In all that we do, whatever choices we have to make, we must take more notice of God. We must come to the realization deep within our hearts with all humility that God is the one who can best control all the affairs of our lives. Trusting God enables him to respond to us in a powerful way and we will continually be refreshed.

- We are challenged to live a life of constant communion with God.

- We are challenged to allow God's law and his commandments to be our rule of faith, allowing those instructions to govern our lives.

- We are challenged to submit ourselves to all that encompasses the divine law. This will ensure good success, long life and prosperity. As the grace of God increases in our lives so will the peace of God.

- We are challenged to have a healthy attitude toward the promises of God, believing that what he speaks he is able to complete.

- We are challenged to have full confidence in the wisdom and power of God, believing that he is wise enough to do what is best for us.

- We are challenged to acknowledge that there is a guiding hand from God, ready to direct and advise us of the course we need to take. God's way is fair and our eyes must be ever focused upon him. Any man who puts himself under divine guidance will always benefit from God's wisdom.

I dare you to be that man!

Prayer of Submission

Father help me to live in humble subjection to your will
For you are sovereign Lord of my life.
Help me to blend completely into your will
Having full confidence in you
Knowing that your hand will guide me
And your grace will see me through
In Jesus Mighty name,
Amen.

CHAPTER 9

THE EFFECT THAT SUBMISSION TO GOD HAS IN OUR SPHERE OF INFLUENCE

> *The LORD told me to give you these laws and teachings, so you can obey them in the land he is giving you. Soon you will cross the Jordan River and take that land. ^{2} And if you and your descendants want to live a long time, you must always worship the LORD and obey his laws. ^{3} Pay attention, Israel! Our ancestors worshiped the LORD, and he promised to give us this land that is rich with milk and honey. Be careful to obey him, and you will become a successful and powerful nation. ^{4} Listen, Israel! The LORD our God is the only true God! ^{5} So love the LORD your God with all your heart, soul, and strength. ^{6} Memorize his laws ^{7} and tell them to your children over and over again. Talk about them all the time, whether you're at home or walking along the road or going to bed at night, or getting up in the morning.*
> (Deuteronomy 6:1-7 CEV)

This chapter teaches us how important it is for a man to teach his children the ways of God so that serving God becomes a way of life. As stated in the earlier part of this book, this passage teaches us to hide the word of God in our hearts that it becomes a source of devotion and obedience to the Lord. Our God wants to continually be near his people, that is why he instructs us to teach our children his word with emphasis on obedience to his will: -

> ^{29}*Oh, that they would always have such a heart for me, wanting to obey my commandments. Then all would go well with them in the future, and with their children throughout all generations!*
> (Deuteronomy 5:29 TLB)

The word that is committed to us must be carefully transmitted to those that follow after us. We must become so familiar with the word that we may have it ready to help guard us against any occasion to sin. God wants us to teach our children so that his word greets them at every turn. This will ensure continual focus on God, which will cause us to regularly check that we continually walking in his ways.

Let the word (spoken by) Christ [the Messiah] have its home [in your hearts and minds] and dwell in you in all its richness, as you teach and admonish and train one another in all insight and intelligence and wisdom [in spiritual things, and sing] psalms and hymns and spiritual songs making melody to God with [His] grace in your hearts. (Colossians 3:16 TAB)

The word of God must saturate our lives and remain in us as a rich treasure. It must dwell within us.

- ❖ We must take our direction and instruction from the word of God.
- ❖ We must become fully acquainted with the word of God.
- ❖ The word of God will dwell in us richly when we have super abundance of it on the inside of us.
- ❖ When adhered to the word of God will make us good Christians and will enable us to conduct ourselves well in everything we do. Psalms and hymns will flow from a heart that is saturated with God's word.

Jesus answered, "The Scriptures say: 'No one can live only on food. People need every word that God has spoken." (Matthew 4:4 CEV)

Divine revelation is required in order to understand God's thoughts and ways. The Bible is the rule and standard of God given to man. When we adhere to its truths we find favour with God. If we refuse to accept its truths then the consequences will be very serious indeed.

What does the word do for us?

Through Scripture and the inspiration of the Holy Spirit, man may discover: -

a) The knowledge of God
b) The nature of God
c) The thoughts of God
d) God's will for human conduct

The word of God corrects us, directs us, and instructs us. Those who trust in God are able to know how to conduct their daily lives.

Young men likewise exhort to be sober-minded. (Titus 2:6)

This scripture outlines the duty of the older men towards the younger men. Young men are known to be eager and passionate, thoughtless and rash. They need encouragement to be considerate and not rash. They also need to be submissive with a teachable spirit and not stubborn and headstrong. Young men need to have self-control in everything.

It is essential that those doing the exhorting/teaching are good examples themselves. Let those you exhort see an active reflection of those same virtues and graces in your life. Once they see your example it will be much easier for them to adhere to the things you are teaching them.

Rely on the wisdom of God

Moses' father-in-law observed him counselling all of the Children of Israel from morning until night and was horrified at the enormity of the job he had undertaken. He made a suggestion that was to prove invaluable to Moses which demonstrated that he had the wisdom of God:-

Moreover thou shalt provide out of all the people able men, such as fear God, men of truth, hating covetousness; and place such over them, to be rulers of thousands, and rulers of hundreds, rulers of fifties, and rulers of tens: (Exodus 18:21)

You will need to appoint some competent leaders who respect God and are trustworthy and honest. Then put them over groups of ten, fifty, a hundred, and a thousand. (Exodus 18:21 CEV)

If thou shalt do this thing, and God command thee so, then thou shalt be able to endure, and all this people shall also go to their place in peace. (Exodus 18: 23)

We do not need to be clever and use our own intellectual approach to win men or to transform society to Jesus Christ. What we do need is the wisdom and understanding of God to guide us. Walking in the awesomeness of God's power will make great impact wherever you tread.

CHAPTER 10

TEN COMMANDMENTS .... TEN CHALLENGES

And God spake all these words, saying, I am the Lord thy God, which have brought thee out of the land of Egypt, out of the house of bondage. Thou shalt have no other gods before me. (Exodus 20:1-3)

The Ten Commandments are laws of God's divine making. They are instructions that God gave which we must carefully adhere to. Applying God's commandments to our lives will enable wisdom, knowledge and understanding to be imparted. We will also receive direct response from God who will put us on the right road to bring society, nations, communities, and families into a new dimension of living under an open heaven.

The first four of the Ten Commandments concern our duty and relationship to God. Our duty to God is to worship him. We worship him inwardly with our affections and love. We worship him outwardly by our acts of obedience to his word.

The first commandment concerns the object of our worship, God himself.

Thou shalt have no other gods before me.

The Egyptians, and other neighboring nations, had many gods and this law was put in place because of that transgression. Jehovah, being the God of Israel, required his people to cleave to him and not to any other god either of their own invention or those borrowed from their neighbours. Each man is to give all glory and honour to God. No other creature should receive what is due to God alone. God alone must be the central figure in our lives. We are not to worship any graven image for we are made in God's image after his likeness as according to Acts 17: 28a: -

It is in him we live and move and have our being.

Pride makes a god of self; covetousness makes a god of money. Whatever is valued, loved, delighted in or depended on more than God in effect becomes our god. I urge you to take the Lord for your God, acknowledge that he is God, accept him in your life, adore him and set your affections entirely upon him.

The second commandment concerns the ordinances of worship, or the way in which God should be worshipped.

Thou shalt not make unto thee any graven image, or any likeness of any thing that is in heaven above, or that is in the earth beneath, or that is in the water under the earth: Thou shalt not bow down thyself to them, nor serve them: for I the LORD thy God am a jealous God, visiting the iniquity of the fathers upon the children unto the third and fourth generation of them that hate me; And shewing mercy unto thousands of them that love me, and keep my commandments. (Exodus 20: 4-6)

Our act of worship must be governed by the power of faith not by the power of imagination. We must not make such images or pictures as the heathen worshipped. Those who desire to be kept from sin must keep themselves from the worship of images. They must not bow down to them on any occasion, that is, show any sign of respect or honour to them. There must be absolute devotion to the one true God, the creator of heaven and earth. No other image should be used for directing or assisting of our personal devotion. It would not please God if we came to him through an image. As the first commandment requires the inward worship of affection and love, so the second requires the outward worship of prayer, praise and serious attendance to God's divine word. Those that truly love God will endeavour to keep his commandments, particularly when it comes to worship. They will receive the grace to keep his other commandments. True worship will cause you to walk in complete obedience to God; the deeper the relationship, the greater the grace.

The third commandment concerns the manner of our worship.

Thou shalt not take the name of the Lord thy God in vain. (Exodus 20:8)

This command gives a needful caution not to mention the name of God in vain, which is still in force today. We take God's name in vain by hypocrisy, making a career of God's name, not living up to our profession, and such like. Those that name the name of Christ but do not depart from iniquity as that name binds them to do, name it in vain. If we make promises to God and do not perform those vows, we take his name in vain. By using the name of God lightly and carelessly, and without any regard, the name of God is taken in vain. God will himself be the avenger of those that take his name in vain.

The fourth commandment concerns the time of worship. God is to be served and honoured on a daily basis, but one day in seven was to be particularly dedicated to his honour and spent in his service.

"Remember the Sabbath day to keep it holy. Six days shalt thou labour, and do all thy work: But the seventh day is the Sabbath of the Lord thy God: in it thou shalt not do any work, thou, nor thy son, nor thy daughter, thy manservant, nor thy maidservant, nor thy cattle, nor thy stranger that is within thy gates: (Exodus 20: 8-10)

This day was to be a day of rest. The Children of Israel were not to do any manner of work on this day whatsoever. This day was to be spent in the presence of God as a holy day, set apart to honour and glorify him. This was a time for them to shut off from everything around them and commune with God. Who were supposed to observe it? *"Thou, and thy son, and thy daughter."* The wife is not mentioned because she was supposed to be one with the husband and present with him, and, if he set apart that day, it is taken for granted that she to would join in with him; but the rest of the family are specified. It is expected that the fathers should not only serve the Lord themselves, but that their households should also serve him.

The last six of the Ten Commandments, addresses our relationships with one another. It is from them that the second greatest commandment stems, *"Thou shalt love thy neighbour as thyself"*. The fifth commandment concerns the duties we owe to our parents:-

Honour thy father and thy mother: that thy days may be long upon the land which the LORD thy God giveth thee. (Exodus 20:12)

Parents should be treated with the respect that is due to them. This includes taking care of them when the need arises such as in sickness and old age. Obedience to this commandment brings the promise that: -

"That thy days may be long in the land which the Lord thy God giveth thee".

The sixth commandment states simply,

"Thou shalt not kill." (Exodus 20: 13)

Man should not do any thing hurtful or injurious to the health of his (her) own or anyone else's life. It forbids all malice and hatred to any person, and all personal revenge arising from all hasty anger, which comes when you are provoked and hurt.

It takes the grace of God in the life of a man to enable a right relationship with a neighbour. The grace that God gives causes us to react in the right way in any situation.

> **FATHER, GIVE ME MORE GRACE THAT I MAY BE GOVERNED BY YOUR WORD. AMEN.**

The seventh commandment addresses our chastity: -

"Thou shalt not commit adultery". (Exodus 20.14)

Our chastity should be as dear to us as our lives; we should therefore guard it jealousy.

Proverbs teaches us to drink water out of our own cistern. Cherish what you have. Your wife is for life, therefore cherish her and love her. Learn to be sensitive to her needs. Support and encourage her. This will go a long way in developing a healthy relationship. A man who is not yet married should learn to wait upon the Lord to ensure that his intensions are honourable in the sight of God.

The eighth commandment concerns our wealth, estate and goods: -

"Thou shalt not steal". (Exodus 20: 15)

This commandment forbids us to take what does not belong to us. Stealing can destroy a life. The effect it has on the victim can be devastating. We should let grace and truth reign in our hearts enabling us to do what is right.

The ninth commandment prohibits lying about another person: -

"Thou shalt not bear false witness." (Exodus 20:16)

This includes speaking unjustly against them to the prejudice of his/her reputation; laying to his/her charge things that he/she knows nothing about; slandering, backbiting, tale-bearing or seeking to raise our own reputation by destroying or ruining another's. Let this not be named among us. We must stand for justice and truth.

The tenth commandment prohibits us from envying anything that belongs to someone else:-

Thou shalt not covet thy neighbour's house, thou shalt not covet thy neighbour's wife, nor his manservant, nor his maidservant, nor his ox, nor his ass, nor any thing that is thy neighbour's. (Exodus 20: 17)

The last three commandments implicitly prohibit doing anything that will cause an injury to others. This commandment forbids excessive desire to have what belongs to someone else. The Apostle Paul, when the grace and power of God caused the scales to fall from his eyes, perceived that this law, *"Thou shalt not covet",* taught him to stand against all those irregular appetites and desires which are the first-born of the corrupt nature. May God give us eyes to see our face in the glass of this law and help us to lay our hearts under the government of it!

I DARE YOU TO….

Dedicate and consecrate your life to God.

Love the Lord God with all your heart, soul, mind, and strength.

Obey and keep the commandments of the Lord God.

Never turn away from serving God.

Meet and commune with God daily.

Submit to the correction of the Holy Spirit.

God wants to pour himself into every man so that his divine nature can sweep this land. There is nothing wrong with submitting ourselves to God for it is in so doing that we will impact the land and bring much needed change to communities, families, nations, and the world.

DISCIPLINE ME LORD (A PRAYER FROM THE HEART)

Father, I humbly bow the knee before your presence
Requesting your discipline in my life.
Though it be painful, purge me Lord
Search and cleanse my innermost being.

Expose my sin, expose my motives and attitudes that are not pure.
Destroy any thoughts, any actions that are not pleasing to you.

Teach me to submit myself to your correction
That I can be in your likeness
And be a full manifestation of your glory

Help me to listen when you speak
Train me, instruct me, that I can live and move
In your power and might.

Help me to trust you
Strengthen and build my faith in you
Help me to recognise that you are the ultimate provider
Let my dependence be only on you.
Your power is impregnable, infallible, unlimited,
None can equal it.
Father I humbly bow the knee before your presence
Hear my prayer.

© *R. C. Francis*
(Used by permission)

CONCLUSION

Becoming the man that God wants us to be is a matter of choice. Life is full of choices. Our aim should be to become the man God wants us to be so that we can affect our world positively.

The challenge is tough, but the rewards are great. Let us begin to change now because the future depends on it!! I dare you to **BE THAT MAN.**

PRAYER SECTION

Prayer To Be A Man Of God

"Blessed are the pure in heart for they shall see God".
(Matthew 5:8)

Father in heaven, my desire is to be the man you want me to be
In your image after your likeness
Teach me how to humble myself before you
I pray that my steps will be ordered of you my God.

I pray that you will train my heart to deal wisely in every situation.
That I will be able to say the right thing at the right time
In the right way.
I pray for the grace to walk in love at all times.
I pray for boldness to refuse the cravings of the flesh and anything
That is not of you, oh heavenly Father.

I pray that the words of my mouth and the meditation of my heart
Will be acceptable in thy sight.
I pray that you will enable me to bring my body under subjection to
Thy will my God.
I pray that I will submit to your authority o heavenly Father.

I pray that I will surrender to the presence and power of the Holy Spirit.
Give me a listening ear that I may hear and respond to your voice,
My Father in heaven.

I desire to be the man you want me to be O Lord, lead me in thy
Way everlasting.
I pray that I will be a man of prayer.
For I know that I am blessed and highly favoured

In Jesus mighty name. Amen.

Prayer For Your Wife

Key Verse

Husbands love your wives, even as Christ also loved the church, and gave Himself for it. (Ephesians 5:25)

Father in heaven, I confess today that you have been good to me.
I thank you that I have been given favour from you and that your blessing is upon my household.
I thank you with all my heart for the beautiful wife that you have blessed me with.
I pray that you will teach me to value her, love and cherish her and acknowledge that she is bone of my bones and flesh of my flesh.
I pray that even when she is sick you will give me the strength to support and comfort her.

It is my desire to treat her with the respect and honour she deserves and I pray that we will become intimately acquainted with one another more deeply than we have ever done before.
Father I pray that she will be covered with your glory and that your blessing will be upon her at all times.

I pray that I will love her as Christ loved the church and gave himself for it.
Father I thank you for giving me such a beautiful, wonderful wife for she is blessed and highly favoured.

In Jesus mighty name. Amen.

Prayer For Your Children

Key Verse

"And all thy children shall be taught of the Lord and great shall be the peace of thy children". (Isaiah 54:13)

Father in heaven, I thank you for the beautiful child/children you have blessed me with.
I thank you for the joy and pleasure they bring around the home.
I speak blessings over their lives.
I pray that the relationship I have with my child/children will be one of honesty, caring and sharing.
I pray that I will make time to spend with them.
I pray that you will cover them with the blood of Jesus.
I pray that prosperity will be their portion.
I pray that they will grow in the grace and in the knowledge of our saviour Jesus Christ
I pray that I will be an example of godliness in the home and exemplify Jesus Christ.
I pray that I will be a reflection of you, Heavenly Father,
And that my children will reflect you also.

My children are blessed and highly favoured
In Jesus mighty name. Amen

A Special Letter

Dear Friend,

While you were reading this book, you may have been wondering whether you too could know God personally and receive his peace in your heart. Jesus said in John 3:3: -

Verily, verily, I say unto thee, Except a man be born again, he cannot see the kingdom of God.

For this to happen in your life, you must…

1. **Acknowledge** to God the Father that you have tried to live independently of him but it has not worked. Romans 3:23. *For all have sinned, and come short of the glory of God.*

2. **Repent** by turning to God and asking for His forgiveness of your past sins and for his help to live as he desires. Luke 13:3. *I tell you, Nay: but, except ye repent, ye shall all likewise perish.*

3. **Believe** that Jesus is the Son of God, and that he died on the cross to take your sin upon himself that you may obtain God's forgiveness. John 3:16. *For God so loved the world, that he gave his only begotten Son, that whosoever believeth in him should not perish, but have everlasting life.*

4. **Confess** to God that you now take Jesus Christ to be Lord and Saviour of your life: Romans 10:9. *That if thou shalt confess with thy mouth the Lord Jesus, and shalt believe in thine heart that God hath raised him from the dead, thou shalt be saved.*

5. **Acknowledge** Jesus Christ as the way, the truth, and the life. John 14:6. *Jesus saith unto him, I am the way, the truth, and the life: no man cometh unto the Father, but by me.*

As the way he is your path to the Father, therefore you cannot be misled.

As the truth he is the reality of all of God's promises, therefore you cannot be deceived.

As the life he joins his divine life to yours both now and eternally. Though you die, you will be alive in him (resurrection).

Would you like to receive Jesus into your life right now? Would you like you sins forgiven? Would you like to be set free to live God's way?

Just repeat this prayer: -

Dear Lord Jesus,

I am a sinner and I want you to save me, I desire you to forgive my sins. I desire you Lord Jesus to come into my heart. Please cleanse me from every sin, deliver me from every habit that has me bound. Heal me. Set me free. Fill my life with your love, your joy and your peace. Lord Jesus I now receive you into my heart. Thank you for taking me as I am. Amen.

You are now a born again believer. Welcome to the family of God!

If you have accepted Jesus as your Lord and Saviour then please write for more information to: -

ries

BTM Life Light
P.O Box 43892
London NW6 5WX

If you require prayer or advice, please write to the above address or e-mail: - ***ministrytomen@aol.com***

To obtain further copies of this book e-mail: -

books@btmlifelight.org

Website: www.btmlifelight.org